Countries Around the World

Egypt

Marta Segal Block

Heinemann Library
Chicago, Illinois

www.capstonepub.com
Visit our website to find out more information about Heinemann-Raintree books.

To order:

☎ Phone 888-454-2279

🖥 Visit www.capstonepub.com to browse our catalog and order online.

© 2012 Heinemann Library
an imprint of Capstone Global Library, LLC
Chicago, Illinois

Edited by Abby Colich and Megan Cotugno
Designed by Philippa Jenkins
Original illustrations © Capstone Global Library, Ltd.
Illustrated by Oxford Designers & Illustrators
Picture research by Liz Alexander
Originated by Capstone Global Library, Ltd.
Printed in China by CTPS

15 14 13 12 11
10 9 8 7 6 5 4 3 2 1

Library of Congress Cataloging-in-Publication Data
Block, Marta Segal.
  Egypt / Marta Segal Block.
    p. cm.—(Countries around the world)
  Includes bibliographical references and index.
  ISBN 978-1-4329-6097-1 (hb)—ISBN 978-1-4329-6123-7 (pb) 1.
Egypt—Juvenile literature. 2. Egypt—History—Juvenile literature. I.
Title. II. Series: Countries around the world (Chicago, Ill.)
  DT49.B56 2012
  962—dc22   2011015259

Acknowledgments
We would like to thank the following for permission to reproduce photographs: The Art Archive: pp. 8 (Collection Antonovich / Gianni Dagli Orti), 10 (Musée du Château de Versailles / Gianni Dagli Orti); Corbis: pp. 20 (© Goran Tomasevic/ Reuters), 24 (© Tara Todras-Whitehill/Reuters), 29 (© Lynsey Addario/VII Network), 34 (© epa); Dreamstime.com: p. 25 (© Markwaters); Getty Images: pp. 7 (Ethan Miller), 12-13: (Hulton Archive), 17 (AFP), 28 (David Silverman), 30 (Cris Bouroncle/ AFP), 36 (Misam Saleh/AFP); Photolibrary: pp. 11 (Steve Vidler), 19 (Henryk T Kaiser); Photoshot: p. 31 (Peter Schickert); Shutterstock: pp. 5 (© bumihills), 21 (© Peter Zaharov), 22 (© Roger De Marfa), 23 (© Uryadnikov Sergey), 27 (© Baloncici), 32 (© Louise Cukrov), 33(© CWB), 35 (© Brandelet), 37 (© Bzzuspajk), 46 (© Sportnet).

Cover photograph of Bazaar at Khan Al-Khalili, Cairo, Egypt, reproduced with permission from Photolibrary (Radius Images).

We would like to thank Shiera S. el-Malik for her invaluable help in the preparation of this book.

Every effort has been made to contact copyright holders of material reproduced in this book. Any omissions will be rectified in subsequent printings if notice is given to the publisher.

Disclaimer
All the Internet addresses (URLs) given in this book were valid at the time of going to press. However, due to the dynamic nature of the Internet, some addresses may have changed, or sites may have changed or ceased to exist since publication. While the author and publisher regret any inconvenience this may cause readers, no responsibility for any such changes can be accepted by either the author or the publisher.

Contents

Some words are printed in bold, **like this**. You can find out what they mean by looking in the glossary.

Introducing Egypt

When many people think of Egypt, they think of things like mummies, pyramids, **hieroglyphics**, the Sphinx, **Pharaohs**, King Tut, and the Nile River.

These are all important parts of this ancient country, but the country is also so much more. Egypt's Nile River has fed people for centuries, providing **papyrus**, the world's first paper, and also the first agriculture. Built in 1970, the Aswan **Dam** remains an important and controversial engineering feat.

Languages of Egypt

The official name of Egypt is the Arab **Republic** of Egypt. In Arabic it is called *Jumhuriyat Misr al-Arabiyah* or *Misr* for short. Although English, French, and German are widely spoken in Egypt, Arabic is the official language. Many Egyptians also speak a language known as "Egyptian Arabic."

Egypt is very important politically. It was the first Arab country to make peace with neighboring Israel. This makes Egypt a valuable friend to countries throughout the world, including the United States.

Visiting Egypt

Located in northern Africa, Egypt is 384,345 square miles (995,450 square kilometers) in size. That's bigger than the state of Texas, but not quite as big as Alaska. Tourism is the country's largest source of foreign money. For centuries people have flocked to this country to see the pyramids and other ancient artifacts.

How to say...
Salaam is the Arabic word for "peace." It is often used as a greeting.

The Nile River has always been essential to Egypt's growth.

History: The Land of the Pharaohs

The Nile River has drawn people to Egypt for centuries. Over 8,000 years ago, hunters and fishers first settled nearby. As they learned to work with the Nile River and its regular patterns of flooding and **drought**, they began to grow certain kinds of grain. Later, they also kept animals.

The Nile River allowed people to travel to other parts of Africa, trading and bringing back ideas. By 3000 BCE, the Nile people were their own **civilization**. The ancient Egyptians also had their own written language known as **hieroglyphics**.

(boot)	B	(snake)	soft G, J	(hand)	hard T, H
(bowl)	K	(twist)	H	(dome)	soft T, H
(hook)	S	(cat)	L	(combs)	long E
(knot)	CH	(owl)	M	(bird)	soft T, H
(pattern)	SH	(eye)	R	(feather)	long U, OO
(hand)	hard S, Z	(zigzag)	N	(bird)	long I short I hard Y
(bar)	D	(square)	P	(bird)	short A short E short O
(worm)	F, V	(bowl with bird)	QU	(sand)	long A
(pot)	hard G	(dome)	T		

This chart shows some common hieroglyphics and their translations.

The Pharaohs

In about 3100 BCE, two kingdoms known as Upper and Lower Egypt united under a powerful leader. This leader came to be known as a **Pharaoh**. The Pharaohs conquered new lands including Nubia (modern-day Sudan), Palestine (modern-day Israel), and Syria.

Although it was unusual in the ancient world, ancient Egyptian women could inherit and own property, and even ask for a divorce. Further, women could become Pharaoh. The earliest female Pharaoh was Meryt-Neith. She was possibly the third Pharaoh and ruled for almost three years. The longest ruling female Pharaoh was Hatshepsut. While the exact years of her rule are difficult to determine, she had power for over 15 years. In portraits Hatshepsut is almost always depicted as a man with a traditional beard.

King Tut (Tutankhamen) is the Pharaoh most famous today, but most historians believe he was a fairly unimportant ruler in his own time.

Alexander the Great

In 332 BCE, Alexander the Great of Macedonia conquered Egypt. Macedonia is near Greece in Europe—not very close to Egypt. Alexander founded the Ptolemy **dynasty** of Pharaohs as well as the city of Alexandria, which he named for himself. Since its founding, Alexandria has been known as an important city for learning.

From Greece to Rome

The last Ptolemy Pharaoh was Queen Cleopatra. Cleopatra tried to attack the **Roman Empire**, but lost. In 31 BCE, Egypt came under Roman rule. Over the next 300 years, Rome changed the Egyptian culture, making Christianity the official religion. The Egyptian Christians were known as Coptics, and many still live in Egypt today.

CLEOPATRA (69 BCE–30 CE)

Cleopatra was a descendant of one of Alexander the Great's generals. She first ruled Egypt with her father and brothers, and later ruled Egypt alone. Although many of the Ptolemy rulers spoke only Greek, Cleopatra learned Egyptian and presented herself as an Egyptian goddess. Today, most people know more about Cleopatra's love life than they know about her as ruler. Cleopatra had children by both Julius Caesar and his general, Marc Antony. Some say her beauty influenced Antony's attempted takeover of Rome. The story of Cleopatra survives in many plays, books, and works of art. She is always portrayed as an amazingly beautiful woman.

Although some sources say Cleopatra was probably not a very beautiful woman, the story of her as a great, beautiful woman survives today.

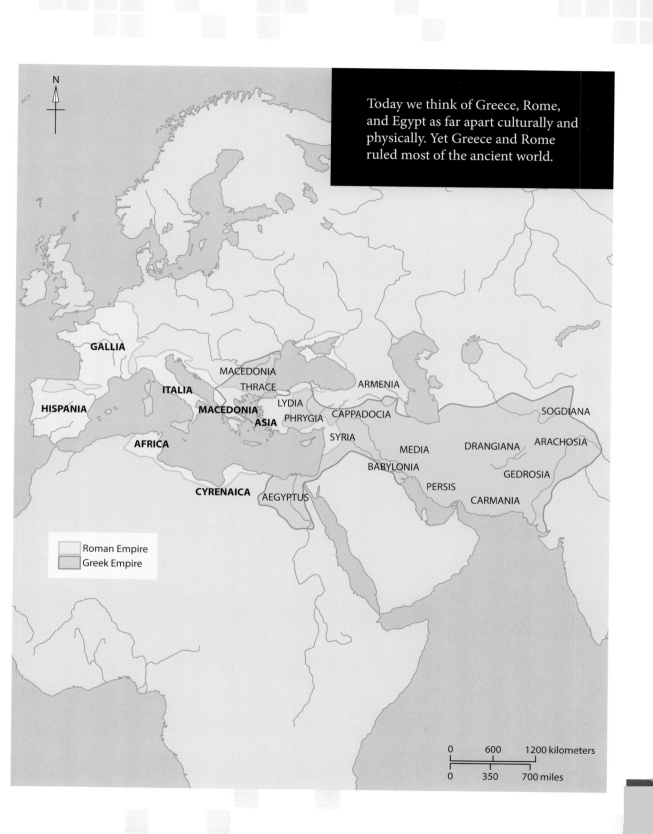

Today we think of Greece, Rome, and Egypt as far apart culturally and physically. Yet Greece and Rome ruled most of the ancient world.

N

GALLIA

MACEDONIA
THRACE
ITALIA
ARMENIA
HISPANIA
MACEDONIA
LYDIA
CAPPADOCIA
SOGDIANA
ASIA
PHRYGIA
AFRICA
SYRIA
DRANGIANA
ARACHOSIA
MEDIA
BABYLONIA
GEDROSIA
CYRENAICA
PERSIS
AEGYPTUS
CARMANIA

Roman Empire
Greek Empire

0   600   1200 kilometers
0   350   700 miles

Islam comes to Egypt

In 640 CE, **Muslim** warriors from the Arabian **Peninsula** took over Egypt and founded the city that today we know as Cairo. **Islam** became the main religion of Egypt and remains so today. For over 200 years, Cairo was the center of the Islamic Empire.

Napoleon and Egypt

In 1517 the Ottoman Empire, based in present-day Turkey, took over Egypt from a group of slave soldiers known as the **Mamluks**. The Mamluks eventually regained power in the 1700s. In 1798 **Napoleon Bonaparte** of France defeated the Mamluks and returned Egypt to the rule of the Ottoman Empire.

Napoleon and his troops before the battle of the pyramids.

Napoleon wanted control of Egypt during the war between France and England. At the time, India was a **colony** of England. Egypt was part of a direct route to India. If France controlled Egypt, then the English would have more trouble traveling to their colony. After conquering Egypt, Napoleon brought Egyptian scholars and artists to France. Much of what we know about ancient Egypt comes from these scholars.

While in Egypt, French troops found the famous Rosetta Stone. The Rosetta Stone is a fragment of an ancient stone. On it is one message written in three ways: in hieroglyphics, in a different form of Egyptian script, and in ancient Greek. The stone made it possible for scholars to **translate** ancient Egyptian hieroglyphics. Today the term "Rosetta Stone" often describes something that is a key to a mystery.

The legendary Rosetta Stone helps us understand ancient Egyptian language and culture.

The Suez Canal

In 1859 Egypt and France built the Suez Canal. The canal is 101 miles (160 kilometers) long and links the Mediterranean Sea and the Red Sea. Before the canal was built, ships went around the tip of Africa to move goods between Asia and Europe. That one-way trip is 4,000 miles (6,435 kilometers)!

The Egyptian government sold its portion of the canal to England in 1869. In 1882 England invaded and took control of Egypt. Then, in 1914, Egypt became a British **protectorate**. Egypt regained some of its independence in 1922 but did not become fully independent for another 30 years.

Independence, war, and peace

In 1952 army officers took control of Egypt and declared it a **republic** with Colonel Gamal Abder Nasser as ruler. Nasser was very popular in the Arab rule. Between 1954 and 2011, Egypt only had three presidents: Nasser, Anwar Sadat, and Hosni Mubarak.

In February 2011, after a series of **riots**, Hosni Mubarak and his entire government were forced to **resign**. The riots were sparked by economic and political turmoil and inspired by a similar revolution in Tunisia. In return, the Egyptian revolution sparked revolutions in other Middle Eastern countries. There is currently an **interim** government.

The Suez Canal allowed traders to cut through Africa, saving time and increasing Europe's influence on Africa.

Regions and Resources: The Land of the Nile

Egypt has four main regions: the Nile Valley and Delta, the eastern region, the western region, and the Sinai **Peninsula**. Egypt is hot and dry all year. The greatest rainfall is in the north—no more than one inch per year—and the rain evaporates quickly in the hot sun. It is hottest in the south, near Aswan. Summer temperatures can rise to 122°F (50°C).

The Nile

The Nile region is only four percent of Egypt's land; however, 99 percent of Egyptians live there. The other one percent is mostly **nomadic Bedouins**. Most of the economic activity in the country takes place in the Nile region. However, the Western Desert has large natural gas and oil **deposits** and offshore oil rigs operate in the Gulf of Suez.

Although tourism is Egypt's most important industry, turquoise, gold, and granite are mined, as are petroleum and natural gas. Corn, wheat, beans, fruits, and vegetables are grown. Farmers rear cattle, water buffalo, sheep, and goats.

How to say...

The ancient Egyptians called the Nile River *Aur* or *Ar*, which means black. Because of the rich, **fertile** soil in the river, the river water looks almost black. Yearly floods of the Nile deposit this dark soil on the banks, allowing Egyptians to grow crops. In modern Arabic, the Nile is called *Nahr an-Nil*.

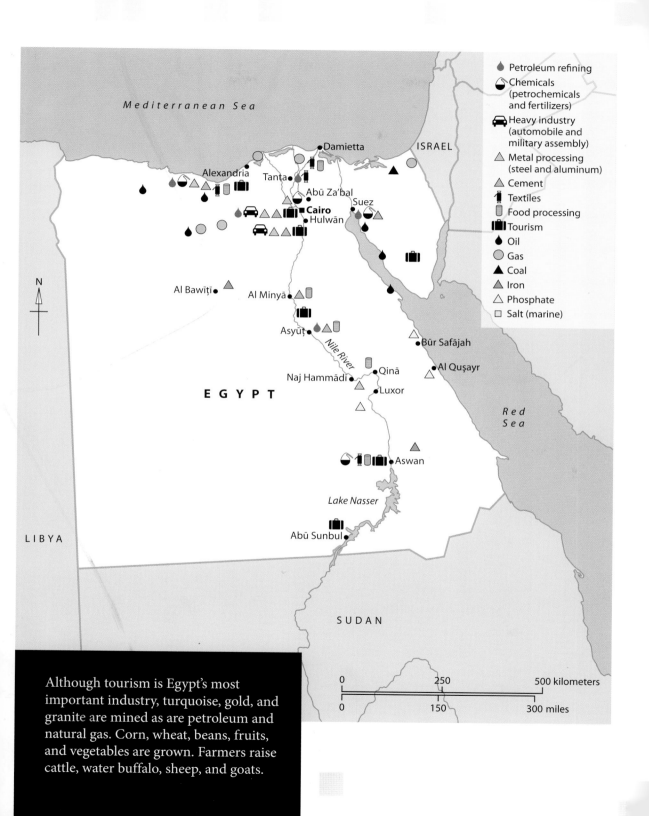

Although tourism is Egypt's most important industry, turquoise, gold, and granite are mined as are petroleum and natural gas. Corn, wheat, beans, fruits, and vegetables are grown. Farmers raise cattle, water buffalo, sheep, and goats.

Aswan High Dam

The city of Aswan is located on the Nile's east **bank**. The stone quarries that provided stones for the ancient pyramids and other statues were located in Aswan.

In 1970 the Aswan High **Dam** was completed. It was thought that the dam would allow farmers to control the Nile and grow crops year-round. However, in addition to storing water, the dam also traps the rich soil of the Nile. This means that the Nile Valley is not as fertile as it used to be.

Pros and Cons of the Aswan High Dam	
Pros	**Cons**
Two or three harvests each year, instead of only one	Dam traps soil, making Nile valley less rich and fertile
Drainage improved	Lower water levels caused collapse of parts of riverbanks
Lives and land saved, thanks to fewer floods	Farmers use too much water since water available year-round
Water available in both Egypt and Sudan in low-water years	Water quality not as good
Lake Nassar has increased fish population, providing important protein source	Increase in weeds because of change in water
High dam power station provides energy	Building of dam forced many people to move

The Aswan High Dam was built over 12 years (1959–1970). The completion was not only a great achievement but also a source of controversy.

The Red Sea

East of the Nile is the Red Sea. No one is certain of the origin of the name "Red Sea." It might refer to the reddish **algae** in the water or to a bordering desert the ancient Egyptians called "Red Desert." The Red Sea is about 1,398 miles (2,250 kilometers) long.

The Sinai

Beyond the Red Sea is the Sinai Desert. Egypt's highest point is known as both Mount Catherine and Mount Sinai. It is 8,625 feet (2,629 meters) high. Tourism is Egypt's most important industry. Because they are significant in the Bible, the Red Sea and Mount Sinai are both major tourist sites.

Western Desert

The Sahara Desert stretches across North Africa. Two thirds of Egypt's land is covered by the desert. This desert is sandy and harder to navigate than the Sinai Desert, but for centuries the nomadic Bedouin people moved across the desert. Today, many Bedouins have settled near the **oases** of the desert.

Mining

Petroleum and natural gas are Egypt's largest mineral resources. Petroleum makes up about one-third of Egypt's **exports**. The Arab Gas Pipeline opened in 2003. It carries natural gas from Egypt to Jordan.

Ancient Bedouins navigated the desert by following desert animals and watching the position of the stars.

Wildlife: Honoring Animals

The ancient Egyptians honored animals. Many of their gods were part human and part animal, and animals were **mummified** after death just as people were. Snakes were feared, but also **revered** as gods. The ancient Egyptians raised animals such as cows and goats, and kept cats as pets. This was very unusual in ancient times.

Camels

Although camels are often seen as a symbol of Egypt and other desert countries, they are not native to the area. In 525 BCE, Persia invaded Egypt and brought the first camels. These Persian camels were not well-suited for trading or traveling over the desert. It wasn't until the 640s that camels became common. The camel is often called the "ship of the desert" because it can carry people and goods.

Today camels are not used very often to cross the desert, but are used for tourist rides and provide meat, milk, wool, and skins.

Camel racing is a popular sport in Egypt.

The hoopoe is one of the most distinctive Egyptian birds. It has black and white wings, a long bill that curves downward, and a large crest on its head.

Birds

There are more than 400 species of birds in Egypt. Many birds stop in Egypt as part of their **migration** from northern Europe to the south of Africa for the winter. But other birds such as eagles and falcons live in the desert and kingfishers, pelicans, and cranes live in and near the swamps and waters.

Marine wildlife

Because very little water enters the Red Sea from the Indian Ocean or from other bodies of water, the Red Sea has its own unique fish. Many of these fish are quite colorful, including the various species of butterfly fish.

There are many species of colorful butterfly fish in Egypt.

The Nile crocodile has a reputation as a vicious people-eater. Crocodiles and humans along the Nile must share a habitat. Nile crocodiles kill about 200 people each year.

Hundreds of years ago you could find hippopotamuses and lions along the **banks** of the Nile. Those animals are no longer present, but the Nile still bursts with life. Perhaps the most famous creature of the Nile is the **endangered** Nile crocodile. The Nile crocodile grows to be about 16 feet (5 meters) long and 500 pounds (227 kilograms). Mummified crocodiles and crocodile eggs have been discovered in ancient Egyptian tombs. This shows that the Egyptians thought the crocodiles were important.

Endangered species

Egypt has 21 regions where animals are protected. Regions include **oases**, deserts, mountains, costal areas, and wetlands. But, because of shrinking deserts, many species in Egypt are losing their natural **habitats**. Endangered species include the sand cat, Nubian ibex (a type of wild goat), dalmation shark, and golden hamster. Birds and water animals are also endangered by human creations such as the Aswan **Dam** and Suez Canal. Animals that have been endangered because of the dam and the canal include the white-headed duck, Nile crocodile, greater spotted eagle, Egyptian tortoise and cape shark.

Infrastructure: A Government in Transition

Officially, Egypt has been a **parliamentary** democracy for years. The government held regular elections and voting was **compulsory**, meaning everyone was required to vote. But in practice, Egypt was actually a dictatorship.

From 1981 to 2011, the government was led by Hosni Mubarak. There was only one **political party** and until 2005, only one person ever ran for president. In 2005, for the first time, rules were changed so that more than one person and party could run for president. However, the rules were so difficult that most people did not think that the elections were fair.

The 2005 elections were the first Egyptian elections to have more than one political party.

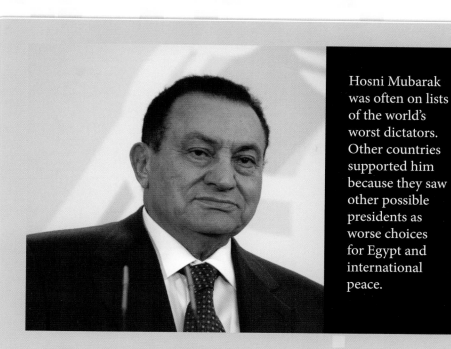

Hosni Mubarak was often on lists of the world's worst dictators. Other countries supported him because they saw other possible presidents as worse choices for Egypt and international peace.

HOSNI MUBARAK (B. 1928)

In 1981 Anwar Sadat was **assassinated**, and Hosni Mubarak became president. Mubarak had been Sadat's vice president, responsible for the country's day-to-day business. Many of Sadat's policies, including making peace with Israel, had been Mubarak's ideas. After Sadat's murder, Mubarak kept most of the policies in place. As Egypt's leader, Mubarak survived six assassination attempts, but his presidency could not survive the revolutionary fever that gripped Egypt in the early days of 2011.

Mubarak held on to power very tightly. He was often referred to as a **dictator** outside of Egypt. Mubarak was especially concerned about Islamists, or Islamic **fundamentalism**. Islamic fundamentalists want the country to be run according to ancient **Muslim** law (known as Sharia law). Islamists often resort to **terrorism** to try and influence politics.

In 2011 a revolution forced Mubarak out of power. Before leaving he attempted to make **concessions**, but by that time it was too late and the Egyptian people demanded he leave.

The future government

What kind of government Egyptians will elect in the coming years is very unclear. Many people believe that the Egyptian people feel angry toward the United States and European powers for their past support of Mubarak. These people worry that Egyptians will elect a government that supports Muslim fundamentalism.

Egypt has always been an important Middle Eastern **ally** for the United States and other Western powers. It is unclear what effect a government that is hostile to these powers will have on relationships.

Egypt's economy

The monetary unit of Egypt is known as the Egyptian Pound (EGP). The Nile Valley has always been the central economic force of Egypt. But, from 2004 to 2008 President Mubarak tried to create **reforms** that would attract foreign investors. Much of Egypt's current economy is dependent on tourism. The global economic crisis that began in 2009 has slowed Egypt's growth. Even during the best parts of Egypt's economic history, living conditions for most have been poor.

Health care

Egypt's growing population is putting a strain on its health care system. As in many countries, health care is provided by a variety of groups including government agencies, nonprofits, and private organizations. Religious organizations are a growing provider of health care in the country.

Life expectancy in Egypt is 75 years for women and 70 years for men. The most common diseases in the country are those associated with living near the water including bacterial diarrhea, typhoid, Rift Valley fever, and schistosomiasis, a disease caused by a parasite.

Like many parts of the world, poor Egyptians do not always benefit from good economic conditions, but suffer during bad ones.

Education

For centuries, Alexandria was known as the center of knowledge of the Ancient world. Egypt has a reputation as an educated country and is home to many universities including Al-Azhar, which was founded in 970 CE.

Approximately 33 percent of Egypt's population is under the age of 15, making education an important issue in the country. Over 71 percent of the population can read. The government provides free education for 11 years, or up to college level. But in many families, children leave school at age 12 to help out with a family business or farm.

These Egyptian children are on a field trip to an Egyptian military museum.

In contrast to many other Islamic countries, girls in Egypt are encouraged to stay in school.

YOUNG PEOPLE

Boys and girls both go to school in Egypt, and the government urges girls to stay in school longer and delay having children. Children in Egypt study the same subjects as children in the United States or England.

Culture: The Heart of Egypt

Islam is the official religion of Egypt. According to the constitution, all laws must agree with Islamic law. Yet, the constitution bans the existence of religious **political parties**. About 90 to 95 percent of Egyptians are **Muslim**, but Egyptian Christians, known in Egypt as Coptics, are also an important part of society. In fact, Egyptian Muslims and Christians get along well. There is also a small number of Egyptians who are of Jewish or Baha'i faith.

In many Muslim countries, women have few rights and must wear traditional Muslim clothing, including veils. In Egypt, however, women have more freedoms than the women living in other Muslim countries. Still, the Egyptian police often ignore cases in which women say their husbands are **abusive**.

This woman is working on the restoration of an Egyptian **synagogue**. There are very few synagogues in Egypt.

The Bedouins

A small but significant part of Egypt's population is **Bedouin**, an early group of Arabs who live in the desert. Many still live in traditional ways, in tents and traveling through deserts, but others have begun to settle in a single location—even in the larger cities. Traditional Bedouin men wear layered and flowing robes. They also wear cloths around their heads and necks as defense against the hot desert sun and wind. Women wear black dresses with head covers. Today, most Bedouin children wear modern clothing.

Many Bedouins are choosing to settle into modern life rather than live the traditional **nomadic** life.

Food in Egypt

Islam forbids eating pork, and cows are not generally kept in Egypt. Therefore, lamb and chicken are the most popular meats. Because of the Aswan **Dam**, fish have also become a popular source of protein.

Traditionally, Egyptians eat family dinners at home, but street vendors everywhere sell quick dishes such as *falafel*, or fried chickpea balls. Western-style fast food restaurants are now more popular and have changed the way people eat.

Egypt's market places are usually crowded with both tourists and locals. Markets specialize in items such as food or cloth.

Daily Life

A typical Egyptian meal starts with a collection of small dishes, called *mezzes*. Choices might include *hummus*, a chickpea-based spread, or *tabbouleh*, a salad with cracked wheat, parsley, and tomatoes. The *mezzes* are often followed by a main course of mixed grilled meats or seafood—or vegetarian choices. Sweets such as *baklava*, made of nuts and honey, and other desserts made of grains and fruits are popular desserts in Egypt.

Cucumber and Chickpea Salad

Salads such as this one are enjoyed around Egypt. Have an adult help you make this recipe.

Ingredients

- 2 cans chickpeas (also called garbanzo beans), drained
- 1 cup chopped tomatoes
- ½ cup minced onions
- ½ cup sliced celery
- 1 cucumber sliced and chopped
- 2 teaspoons of minced garlic
- 1 teaspoon dill
- 3 teaspoons red wine vinegar
- ½ cup olive oil

Method

1. Mix oil and vinegar and set aside.
2. Combine all other ingredients, and then toss with the vinegar and oil mixture. Put the salad in the refrigerator for about an hour before serving.

Hollywood of the Arab world

Cairo is considered the Hollywood of the Arab world, turning out movies that are popular worldwide. Cairo is also the heart of Egypt's television stations; however, Egyptians with satellite TVs watch broadcasts from around the world, including from Europe and the United States.

AHDAF SOUEIF (B.1950)

Although she writes primarily in English, Ahdaf Soueif is one of the best-known Egyptian authors. Soueif is an outspoken critic of Israel's policies toward Palestinians and also an activist for **gay rights**. She lives in both London and Cairo. Her most famous book is *The Map of Love* (1999).

Egyptian literature has a long history. In 1998 Naguib Mahfouz was the first Egyptian to win a Nobel Prize.

Beautiful coral reefs make the Red Sea one of the most popular destinations for scuba diving.

Sports

As in many Arabic and African countries, soccer—or football, as Egyptians call it—is Egypt's favorite sport. When important matches are played, the country comes to a standstill. Other popular sports include horse riding and racing. Water sports, such as water skiing and rowing, are popular in Egypt. Also popular is sailing in traditional flat-bottomed boats known as *feluccas*. The Red Sea is considered one of the world's best places for scuba diving and snorkeling.

Egypt Today

In 1869 Thomas Cook, one of the first tour organizers, arranged a tour to Egypt. This was the beginning of modern tourism. While Egyptian oil and gas **exports** are significant, tourism is Egypt's main source of income.

Depending on tourism is risky for any country, but it is especially risky for a country in the Middle East. In 2003, when the United States invaded Iraq, tourism in Egypt dropped dramatically. Islamic terrorists have also been known to target Egypt.

Although Egypt's political future is unclear, its place in history and its importance to the world is not. The beginnings of the culture of the modern world are rooted in Egypt. Its art, literature, and politics will continue to affect the entire world.

In 2011 Egyptians rallied against President Hosni Mubarak in Tahir Square in downtown Cairo.

Despite many changes, Cairo continues to thrive as Egypt's largest city.

Fact File

Country Name:	Arab Republic of Egypt
Capital:	Cairo
Language:	Arabic
Religions:	Muslim (90%), Coptic Christian (9%), Other (1%)
Type of Government:	Republic; also considered a dictatorship
Independence Date:	1953
National Anthem:	Bilady, Bilady, Bilady ("My Homeland, My Homeland, My Homeland")

My homeland, my homeland, my homeland,
My love and my heart are for thee.
Egypt! O mother of all lands,
My hope and my ambition,
How can one count
The blessings of the Nile for mankind?

Chorus:
Egypt! Most precious jewel,
Shining on the brow of eternity!
O my homeland, be forever free,
Safe from every foe!

Population:	80,471,869 (est. 2010)
Life Expectancy:	72.4 years
Median Age:	24 years (male: 23.8 years; female: 24.3 years)
Literacy Rate:	74.3% (male: 83.4%, female: 65.3%)
Bordering Countries:	Libya, Sudan, and the Gaza Strip
Total Land Area:	384, 345 square miles (995,450 square kilometers)

Largest Cities:	Cairo (population 7,764,700) Alexandria (population 3,806,300) Giza (population 2,541,000)
Climate:	desert (hot, dry summers with moderate winters)
Major Rivers:	Nile
Highest Elevation:	Mount Catherine (Mount Sinai): 8,625 feet (2,629 meters)
Lowest Elevation:	Qattara depression: -436 feet (-133 meters)
Currency:	Egyptian Pound (EGP)
Resources:	petroleum, natural gas, phosphates, iron ore, lead, zinc
Industries:	textiles, food processing, tourism, chemicals, pharmaceuticals, construction
Imports:	fuels, chemicals, foodstuffs, machinery equipment
Exports:	crude oil and petroleum products, cotton, textiles, chemicals
National Holidays:	January 7 Coptic Christmas January 25 National Police Day April 25 Sinai Liberation Day May 1 Labor Day July 23 Revolution Day October 6 Armed Forces Day
Famous Egyptians:	Amr Diab, singer (b. 1961) Euclid, father of geometry (300s BCE) Karam Gaber, athlete (b. 1979) Mohamed Al Fayed, businessman (b. 1933) Naguib Mahfouz, writer (1911–2006) Omar Sharif, actor (b. 1932) Meriam George, model (b. 1987)

Timeline

BCE is short for Before the Common Era. BCE is added after a date and means that the date occurred before the birth of Jesus Christ, for example, 450 BCE.

CE is short for Common Era. CE is added after a date and means that the date occurred after the birth of Jesus Christ, for example, 720 CE.

BCE

3100	King Menes unites the kingdoms of Upper and Lower Egypt.
c. 2500	The pyramids of Gaza and the Sphinx are built.
525	Persians conquer Egypt.
30	Egypt becomes part of the Roman Empire.

CE

642	Muslim Arabs conquer Egypt.
1517	Ottoman Empire invades Egypt and rules for 300 years.
1798	Napoleon Bonaparte invades Egypt.
1799	Rosetta Stone is discovered.
1869	Suez Canal is finished.
1914	Egypt becomes a British protectorate.
1922	Egypt gains limited independence from Britain.
1952	Army officers led by Gamal Abder Nasser overthrow Egypt.
1953	Egypt is declared a republic.
1967	The Six-Day War occurs.
1970	Aswan High Dam is completed.
1978	Egypt's Anwar Sadat signs peace accord with Egypt.
1981	Sadat is assassinated; Hosni Mubarak becomes president.
2005	Terrorist bombing of Sharm el-Sheikh.
2005	Constitutional amendment allows multiple candidates for president.
2011	Protests break out against economic conditions and President Mubarak resigns.

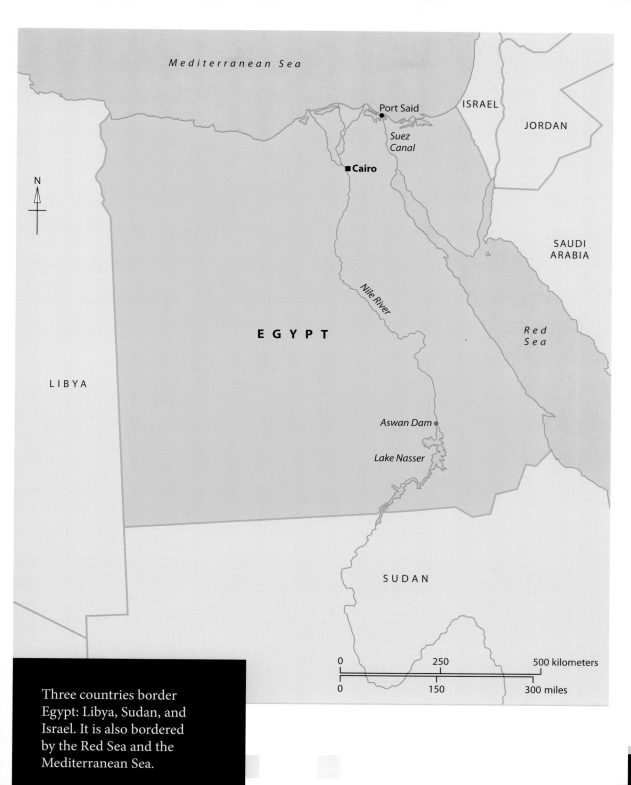

Three countries border
Egypt: Libya, Sudan, and
Israel. It is also bordered
by the Red Sea and the
Mediterranean Sea.

Glossary

abusive act of hurting a person or animal

algae simple plants that don't have stems, roots, or leaves

ally friend

assassinate murder for political reasons

bank side of a river

Bedouin Arab of the desert in Asia or Africa

civilization culture and way of life of a certain group

colony country or territory ruled by an outside power or government

compulsory required by law

concession give something up, as in a compromise

dam something, usually a concrete structure, that holds back water in order to make electricity or to have a water supply

deposit natural accumulation of matter

dictator ruler with total power who often takes power by force

drought long period of little or no rainfall and the water shortage that results

dynasty family that rules a country and passes the power from one generation to the next

endangered at risk of becoming extinct

export something sold or sent to other countries

fertile (regarding land) capable of abundant plant growth

fundamentalism strict belief in a religion, often its ancient form and ideology

gay rights equal opportunities for homosexual people

habitat natural environment for a living being

hieroglyphics ancient Egyptian form of writing that is made up of pictures and symbols

interim temporary; not lasting a long time

Islam religious faith of Muslims, based on the text of the Koran and teachings of the prophet Muhammad

Mamluk in Muslim societies, soldier that was a slave

migration mass movement from one place to another

mummify preserve a dead body by embalming and wrapping in cloth

Muslim follower of Islam, or having to do with a follower of Islam

Napoleon Bonaparte French emperor from 1804 to 1814 and for a short time in 1815

nomad person or group of people who intentionally move from place to place and who are without a permanent home

oases fertile areas in the middle of a desert

papyrus plant that grows along the banks of the Nile; its leaves are used to make paper

Pharaoh ruler in ancient Egypt

parliamentary government in which people elect representatives who then choose a leader

peninsula land surrounded by water

political party organization that wants to influence the government

protectorate country or area under the protection of another country, often following some of the other country's rules, but still maintaining independence in local issues

reform change something for the better

republic form of government in which the people elect their leaders

revere honor or worship

resign leave a job or position

riot noisy, violent public fight caused by a crowd of people

Roman Empire ruling power over much of Europe and Africa lasting from approximately 44 BCE to 476 CE

synagogue religious place for Jewish people

terrorism regular use of violence or threats to achieve a goal

translate change words from one language into another

Find Out More

Books

Bowden, Rob. *Settlements of the River Nile*. Chicago: Heinemann, 2005.

Heinrichs, Ann. *Egypt (Enchantment of the World)*. New York: Scholastic, 2007.

Wood, Selina. *Egypt (Countries of the World)*. Washington D.C.: National Geographic, 2007.

Websites

www.bibalex.org/libraries/presentation/static/13513.aspx
The Library of Alexandria seeks to recapture the spirit of the ancient Library of Alexandria.

www.britannica.com/EBchecked/topic/180382/Egypt
Learn more about Egypt from the Encyclopedia Britannica.

http://kids.nationalgeographic.com/kids/places/find/egypt/
Country facts, information, photos, and videos about Egypt can be found here.

http://www.historyforkids.org/learn/egypt/
Discover ancient Egypt for Kids.

Places to visit

The Great Pyramid of Giza

The largest and oldest pyramid, it was most likely built around 2,650 BCE.

The Sphinx of Giza

The construction and meaning of this ancient statue remains a mystery.

Bedouin Life

Tours can be arranged to see how modern Bedouins live.

The Red Sea

The Red Sea provides excellent snorkeling and scuba diving.

Topic Tools

You can use these topic tools for your school projects. Trace the map onto a sheet of paper, using the thick black outline to guide you.

When Egypt achieved independence many other Arab nations were also fighting for their independence from England. The red, white, and black colors are shared by Iraq, Syria, and Yemen and stand for the struggle. The golden eagle in the middle of the flag is the national symbol of Egypt.

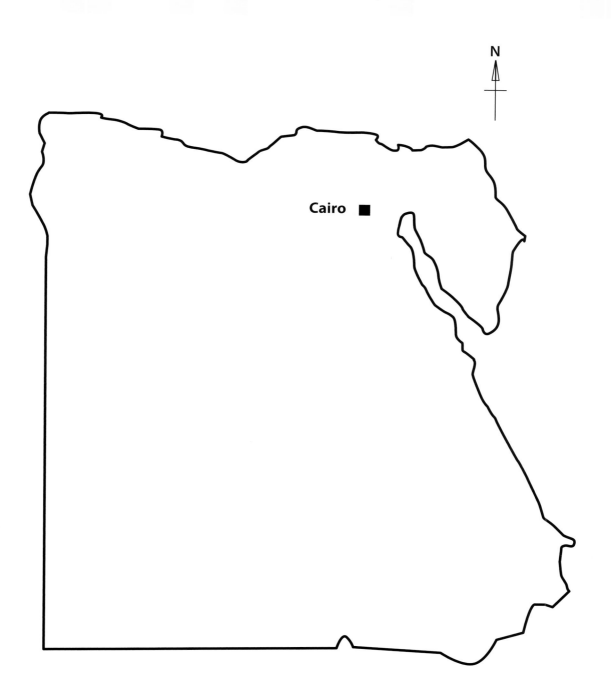

Cairo ■

N

Index